To:

From:

Tie a Yellow Ribbon

Tony Orlando

Rutledge Hill Press®
Nashville, Tennessee
A Division of Thomas Nelson Publishers
www.ThomasNelson.com

Published by Rutledge Hill Press, a Division of Thomas Nelson, Inc., P.O. Box 141000, Nashville, Tennessee 37214.

Rutledge Hill Press books may be purchased in bulk for educational, business, fund-raising, or sales promotional use. For information, please e-mail SpecialMarkets@ThomasNelson.com.

Design by studiogearbox.com

1-4016-0256-8

Printed in Mexico
06 07 08 09 10—5 4 3 2 1

I COULD never have predicted the impact this song, "Tie a Yellow Ribbon," would have on my career—and on my country. When we recorded it in 1973, we hoped for a hit song. It not only became a huge hit, it also became the theme song for the *Tony Orlando and Dawn* television show. This song changed my life, but the greatest inspiration was to see how the song touched so many hearts and lives, becoming an anthem of hope and love for the entire country.

It started with the 1973 Cotton Bowl performance, hosted by Bob Hope and welcoming our POWs home from Vietnam, Cambodia, and Laos. Seventy thousand people were welcoming these brave men, and as we began the chorus, "Tie a yellow ribbon" they started singing the chorus along with us, joining in as if it was a national anthem.

Mr. Hope said to me, "Tony, the opening line of your song, 'I'm coming home, I've done my time,' is every mother's wish, every soldier's prayer; every mother's prayer, and every soldier's wish. You're going to be singing this song for the rest of your life." How prophetic he was. I was just the mailman who delivered the letter, along with the songwriters: in memory of Irwin Levin and special thanks to L. Russell Brown. It has been the greatest privilege of my life to be involved with bringing this song to the world.

"Tie a Yellow Ribbon" welcomed the hostages home from Iran in 1980. Yellow ribbons flew on everything from the space shuttle to sky scrapers. Then people sang the song in support of our troops during Desert Storm. Today driving down the freeway you'll see yellow ribbons on cars in support of our troops in Afghanistan and Iraq. Yellow ribbons have become an icon for those who wait at home for their loved ones far away.

No matter how far away your loved one may be, they are always near and dear to the heart. So we'll tie that yellow ribbon on that oak tree or on our front door or stick it to our car to let them know though they are in our thoughts and prayers and that we love and honor them with all our hearts.

It was about a return from prison.

Then it became a song.

Then it became welcome home from Iran.

Then it was for a lost son or daughter.

Then it was for Desert Storm.

Then it was for a cause.

Now it is for you.

ALWAYS KNOW WHERE HOME IS.

HOPE is the most amazing boat in the world.

Storms cannot sway it,

Deep waters cannot sink it,

Enemies cannot destroy it,

It forever sails into the horizon of the unknown

To bring you home to me.

I watched them all saying good-bye.

Some were loud.

Some were laughing.

Some were crying.

It was as if in slow motion.

Life was happening all around me.

And I just watched, trying to breathe again.

There is the first-day-of-school *good-bye*,

There is the empty-nest *good-bye*,

There is the end-of-summer *good-bye*,

There is the perfect-night-under-the-moon *good-bye*,

There is the unsaid *good-bye*,

There is the stolen *good-bye*,

There is the noble *good-bye*,

THERE IS NO GOOD-BYE THAT COMPARES WITH TODAY.

IT IS ALL ABOUT THE journey.

WE ARE **CREATED** BY IT.

WE ARE MADE **STRONGER** BY IT.

WE ARE **DESTROYED** BY IT.

AND WE ARE **REBORN** FROM IT.

FOR AS FAR AS YOUR ROAD GOES . . .

I'LL BE HERE WHEN YOU RETURN.

If our time apart were measured in heartbeats,

There would be nothing to measure.

My heart stopped the day we said good-bye.

{ IT WILL BEGIN WHEN WE ARE

TOGETHER AGAIN. }

CAN THERE BE

ANY PLACE YOU CAN BE

THAT I AM NOT THERE STILL?

I'll whisper in your heart
And you will know.

A mother waits and cries.

A father worries and comforts.

A wife hopes and hurts.

A child wonders and grows up.

A brother bucks up and pretends.

A sister gets busy and makes scrapbooks.

A friend ... goes fishing at that perfect spot you found
and remembers.

There is an empty place at our table.

We can hardly reach across it to hold hands and say grace.

We bless our homes and bless the supper,

And pass around all your favorite things.

We talk about our days.

We talk about the news.

We talk about each other.

And then we always talk about you.

We find a way to laugh at something
    you used to do.

Dad always gets real quiet,

And mom always has something in the
    kitchen to get to.

We clear the table just like always,
    the plates, the forks, the cups,

And suddenly I realized, you are getting
out of cleaning up the kitchen
Just like you always have!

That old dog sits on the front porch every afternoon and waits.

He hardly notices there's a food bowl out there.

It got cold last night,

And he wouldn't come in.

He's waiting for you.

(I KNOW JUST HOW HE FEELS.)

LONELY is a sea of people

Where everyone is a stranger

Even those who know my name.

It is the space and time between

good-bye and hello . . . And you.

Faith, hope, and love …

That's how I know.

How long does **love** give

before it gives up?

The answer is in the acorn that somehow
gets buried and disappears,
Until one day it is an oak so mighty its branches
reach into the heavens,
And looks as if it has always been.

SO JUST HOW BIG IS A

MUSTARD SEED

ANYWAY?

DO YOU KNOW

HOW FAR YOU WOULD HAVE TO GO TO

GET AWAY FROM MY LOVE?

There is no place that far, my love.

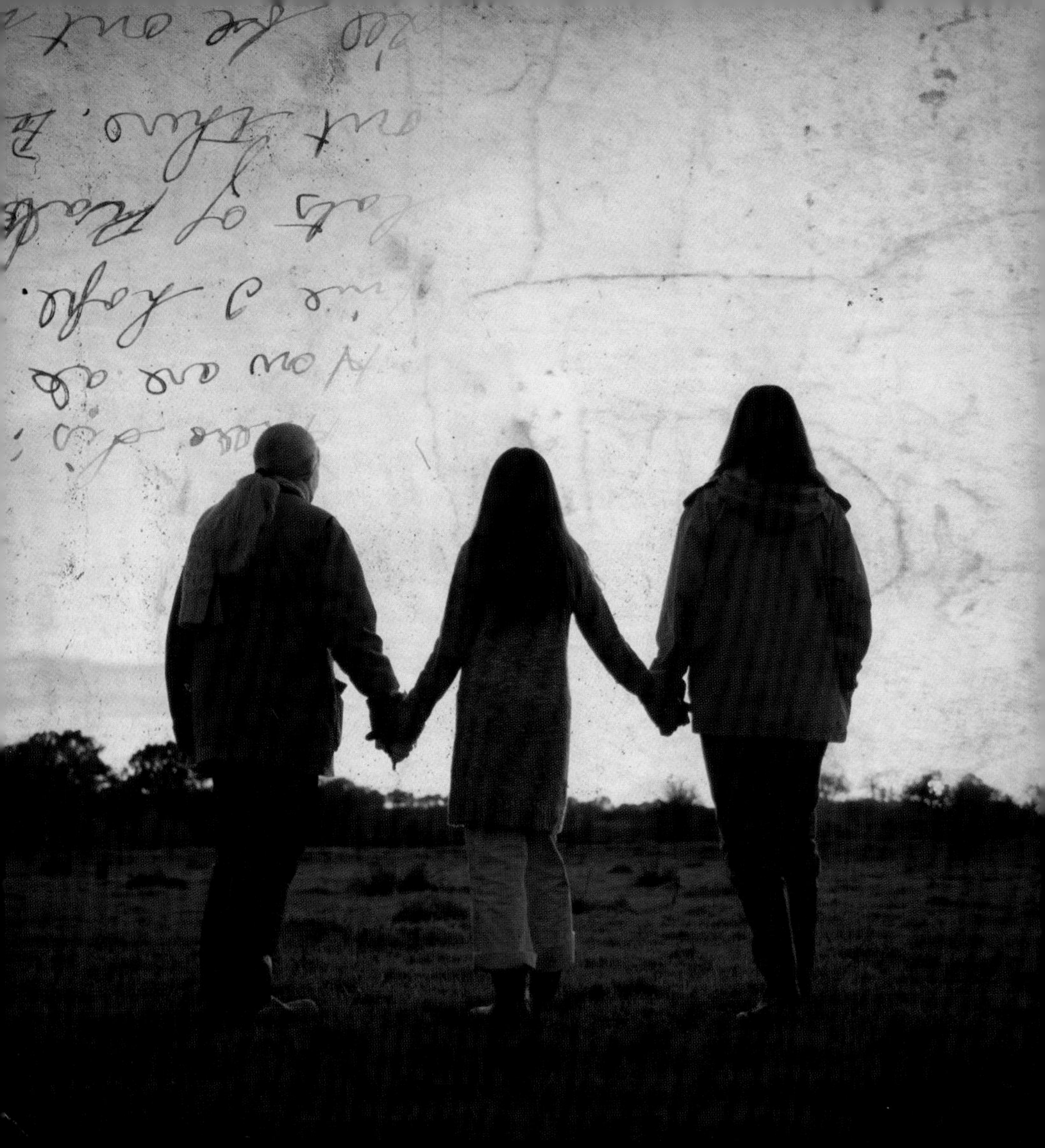

The *mother*, the *wife*, the *daughter*
All sat on a rock talking.

The mother said, "My son is gone, you don't understand"
The wife said, "My love is gone, you don't understand."
The daughter said, "My daddy's gone, you don't understand."
And then they all cried, held each other, and
eventually smiled.

They understood.

Happily ever after

NEVER ADDRESSED YOU THERE

AND ME HERE.

REMEMBER WHEN

LONG DISTANCE

WAS A PHONE CALL,

AND WE NEVER HAD TO USE IT?

Tomorrow, I will take out the trash.

Tomorrow, I will take the kids to school.

Tomorrow, I will try to fix the leaky toilet.

Tomorrow, I will pay the bills that I never knew existed.

Tomorrow, I will learn to use a catcher's mitt for our son.

Tomorrow, I will go to school and have a word with that bully who harrassed our daughter.

Tomorrow, I will go to work and be strong, confident, and a great provider.

Tonight, I will go to sleep alone, shedding the tears I can let no one see.

WHEN THE NIGHT

GETS LONG, DARK,
AND COLD

Wrap my love around you like the softest,
warmest blanket in the world.

No one can carry your baggage up a hill. It gets so heavy.

I want everyone to see it, and take pity on me.

I want the world to know.

I want to kick the person that said "If it doesn't kill me,

it'll make me stronger."

Another e-mail that says "God wouldn't bring you to it,

if He won't bring you through it," and I'll scream.

Doesn't anyone get it? Doesn't anyone believe me?

I'm tired of carrying this.

I've had enough. I've had it.

I'm done.

Ok . . . I'm stronger.

I'll be waiting.

YELLOW

IS THE COLOR FOR COURAGE WHEN YOU ARE WAITING

FOR SOMEONE TO COME HOME.

Write me a letter.

Not some electronic thing,

Not some faraway phone call . . . a letter.

Your hand, paper, a pen, and words.

Write me something I can put under my pillow

And dream on.

Pub. by Max Bernstein, Kansas City, Mo.

Do what you need,

Do what you must,

    I will be here when you get home,

My heart is one to trust.

REAL LOVE DOESN'T CHANGE
WHEN WE ARE APART.

It ages with a picture of our passionate
youth etched in our minds.

WE NEVER GROW APATHETIC.

WE NEVER GROW UP.

WE NEVER GROW OLD.

We stay beautifully in love in our hearts until we meet
again as young lovers who have forever to love.
There is a symbolic cord from your heart to mine.
It reaches around the world and back again connecting us by an
unchangeable love. It shines forever gold like the sun.

In all the things I have ever heard

attributed to love,

the greatest I have found is this:

Love waits.

In a box in the back of the attic,

There is an old love letter.

It is a memory from a time when the words were new.

It has yellowed with age,

But the message is forever.

I love you, too.
xxxooo

For the first time in my life,

I feel like I cannot control this.

I can keep my house in order.

I can keep the bank account straight.

I can keep everyone at work toeing the line.

But I cannot control this.

You aren't here.

I can't go pick you up at a friend's house

and bring you home.

I can't picture where you are.

I can't pick up the phone and call you.

I can't wait and do nothing.

I PRAY.

THE

STRENGTH OF

LOVE

IS NEVER KNOWN,

UNTIL

TESTED BY FIRE.

We have been burned black,
letting the ashes fall,
And all that remains is pure, sweet,
precious, and everlasting.

Take me in your arms

and make me forget.

Take me in your arms and make me remember.

Take me in your arms and heal my brokenness.

Take me in your arms

and make me new.

One day at a time.

That's all we can do,

Trusting that each day is one day closer,

Knowing that each step is one step of forward motion.

Keep walking. Keep trusting. Keep believing. Keep loving.

It is in our journey to love that we are

becoming who we are to be.

I look into your eyes and know

That I am home.

TIE A YELLOW RIBBON

I'm comin' home; I've done my time.
Now I've got to know what is
   and isn't mine.
If you received my letter telin' you
   I'd soon be free,
Then you'll know just what to do
   if you still want me.
If you still want me,

Tie a yellow ribbon round the
   old oak tree.
It's been three long years.
Do you still want me?
If I don't see a yellow ribbon round
   the old oak tree,
I'll stay on the bus,
Forget about us,
Put the blame on me,
If I don't see a yellow ribbon round
   the old oak tree.

Bus driver, please look for me
'Cause I couldn't bear to see what
   I might see.

I'm really still in prison, and my
   love she holds the key.
A simple yellow ribbon's what I
   need to set me free.
I wrote and told her please:

Tie a yellow ribbon round the
   old oak tree.
It's been three long years.
Do you still want me?
If I don't see a yellow ribbon round
   the old oak tree,
I'll stay on the bus,
Forget about us,
Put the blame on me,
If I don't see a yellow ribbon round
   the old oak tree.

Now the whole damn bus is
   cheering,
And I can't believe I see,
A hundred yellow ribbons round
   the old oak tree.
I'm comin' home!